"God delights to turn things upside down. Most think a 'worthy' person must be someone great. Sinclair Ferguson shows that the people 'worthy of the gospel' are those humbled by their sins, transformed by Christ's cross, and obsessed with knowing the Lord. Nothing less is fitting for the gospel. Highly recommended!"

Joel R. Beeke, President, Puritan Reformed Theological Seminary

"Like conjoined twins, legalism and antinomianism share the same heart. Curved in on itself, it recoils at being justified by an alien righteousness and being sanctified by conformity to someone else's identity. Sinclair Ferguson's long ministry of proclaiming God's word has always struck at both forms of heart disease. Laced with pastoral warmth, striking illustrations, and dry Scottish humor, *Worthy* sets the table richly for a feast that will nourish the hearts of believers and invite strangers to pull up a chair."

Michael Horton, J. Gresham Machen Professor of Systematic Theology and Apologetics, Westminster Seminary California

"For years, Sinclair Ferguson has helped me toward having an experiential grasp of my union with Christ. His sermons and books have been friends along the way, leading toward spiritual maturity and a life with God. Because *Worthy* is a short book, I assumed it would be a summary of ideas I've read or heard from Ferguson elsewhere. Instead, each chapter felt full of fresh insights and pastoral wisdom. As I was finishing this book, I kept telling others how excited I am for my congregants and even my teenage children to read it."

John Starke, Lead Pastor, Apostles Church, New York City; author, *The Possibility of Prayer*

T0017004

Worthy

Union

Growing Gospel Integrity

Michael Reeves, series editor

Worthy: Living in Light of the Gospel, Sinclair B. Ferguson

Humility: The Joy of Self-Forgetfulness, Gavin Ortlund

Worthy

Living in Light of the Gospel

Sinclair B. Ferguson

WHEATON, ILLINOIS

Worthy: Living in Light of the Gospel

Copyright © 2023 by Sinclair B. Ferguson

Published by Crossway
   1300 Crescent Street
   Wheaton, Illinois 60187

Cover design: Jordan Singer

First printing 2023

Printed in the United States of America

Trade paperback ISBN: 978-1-4335-8317-9
ePub ISBN: 978-1-4335-8320-9
PDF ISBN: 978-1-4335-8318-6

Library of Congress Cataloging-in-Publication Data

Names: Ferguson, Sinclair B., author.
Title: Worthy : living in light of the gospel / Sinclair B. Ferguson.
Description: Wheaton, Illinois : Crossway, 2023. | Series: Growing gospel integrity | Includes bibliographical references and index.
Identifiers: LCCN 2022038680 (print) | LCCN 2022038681 (ebook) | ISBN 9781433583179 (trade paperback) | ISBN 9781433583186 (pdf) | ISBN 9781433583209 (epub)
Subjects: LCSH: Jesus Christ—Example.
Classification: LCC BT304.2 .F47 2023 (print) | LCC BT304.2 (ebook) | DDC 232.9/04—dc23/eng/20221209
LC record available at https://lccn.loc.gov/2022038680
LC ebook record available at https://lccn.loc.gov/2022038681

Crossway is a publishing ministry of Good News Publishers.

VP		31	30	29	28	27	26	25	24	23
14	13	12	11	10	9	8	7	6	5	4	3	2	1

To
Derek and Rosemary
in gratitude
for
our friendship
and
your ministry

*Only let your manner of life be
worthy of the gospel of Christ.*

PHILIPPIANS 1:27

Contents

Series Preface

GOSPEL INTEGRITY IS, I suggest, the greatest and most vital need of the church today. More than moral behavior and orthodox beliefs, this integrity that we need is a complete alignment of our heads, our hearts, and our lives with the truths of the gospel.

In his letter to the Philippians, the apostle Paul issues a call to his readers to live as people of the gospel. Spelling out what this means, Paul sets out four marks of gospel integrity.

First, he entreats, "let your manner of life be worthy of the gospel of Christ" (1:27a). The people of the gospel should live lives *worthy* of the gospel.

Second, this means "standing firm in one spirit, with one mind striving side by side for the faith of the gospel" (1:27b). In other words, integrity to the gospel requires a *united* stand of faithfulness together.

Third, knowing that such a stand will mean suffering and conflict (1:29–30), Paul calls the Philippians not to be "frightened in anything" (1:28a). He describes this *courage* as "a clear sign" of our salvation (1:28b).

Fourth, Paul writes:

> So if there is any encouragement in Christ, any comfort from love, any participation in the Spirit, any affection and sympathy, complete my joy by being of the same mind, having the same love, being in full accord and of one mind. Do nothing from selfish ambition or conceit, but in humility count others more significant than yourselves. (2:1–3)

Paul thus makes it clear that there is no true Christian integrity without *humility*.

The simple aim of this series is to reissue Paul's gospel-based call to an integrity that means living *worthily*, *unitedly*, *courageously*, and *humbly*. We need to recognize, however, that these four marks are not abstract moral qualities or virtues. What Paul has in mind are, quite specifically, marks and manifestations *of integrity to the gospel*. As such, the books in this series will unpack how the gospel fuels and shapes those qualities in us.

Through this little series, may God be glorified, and may "the grace of the Lord Jesus Christ be with your spirit" (4:23).

Michael Reeves
Series Editor

Introduction

THE TITLE OF THIS LITTLE BOOK—*Worthy*—cries out for explanation for one obvious reason: generations of Christians, stretching back into Bible times, have always affirmed that while God is worthy, we are not. Nevertheless, it was the apostle Paul—a man deeply conscious of both his own unworthiness and the wonder of God's grace and mercy—who urged his fellow Christians to live in a way that is *worthy*.

So these pages are about being "worthy" of the gospel—an exhortation Paul gave to some of his favorite fellow-believers in the church at Philippi.

In writing this book I have frequently found myself asking, "Since Paul urges his correspondents to 'live lives worthy of the gospel,' does he explain what this means and how it happens?" If we meditate on what he says, we will discover that—sometimes in low-key ways—he explains more fully what his exhortation means, how he experienced its fulfillment himself, and how we can as well.

So while *Worthy* is not meant to be an exposition of the letter to the Philippians, we will regularly find ourselves reflecting on what Paul says there. In fact, at the time he wrote, urging Christians to be worthy of the gospel seems to have been a special burden on his heart. He also mentioned it in his letters to the Ephesians and the Colossians, written around the same time. And he had already emphasized it in his first letter to the Thessalonians.

So, clearly this was not an incidental or a peripheral matter to him. Perhaps he knew that being worthy had also been a burden on his Savior's heart for his disciples. For did he not say: "Whoever loves father or mother more than me is not worthy of me. . . . And whoever does not take his cross and follow me is not worthy of me" (Matt. 10:37–38)?

So being *worthy* turns out to be the sure mark of Jesus's disciples. True, at first sight Paul's words "*only* let your manner of life be worthy" might seem to suggest that it is incidental. But it isn't a casual afterthought in Paul's mind. In fact, as we will see, he gives it the highest priority.

I wonder if you would agree with me when I say that I don't think Christians give it the same priority today. It is just possible that you have never heard a sermon or a lesson on

Paul's words, and even less likely that you have read a book (even a short one like this!) on being worthy.

But that surely means it is all the more important that we hear what Paul says.

———

Worthy is part of a short series of books devised by Michael Reeves on the basis of Paul's words in Philippians 1:27–2:3. *Worthy* both introduces and summarizes their main theme. I am grateful for the invitation to contribute to the series, and I hope this volume will serve as an encouragement to you to read the other three. More than that, I hope it will remind you of an exhortation that has too often been forgotten.

Be Worthy

A Forgotten Calling?

"ONLY LET YOUR MANNER OF LIFE be worthy of the gospel of Christ" (Phil. 1:27).

That word "only" might deceive us into thinking this is a casual statement, like "Wait for me, I'll *only* be a minute or two."

But, in fact, it is the reverse. There is nothing casual here. When Paul says "only," he uses the Greek word *monon*. Even if you have no knowledge of Greek, you can probably guess its meaning. "Only" here means "one and only," "the one thing needful." "*Only* let your manner of life be worthy of the gospel of Christ" means this is a nonnegotiable.

Yet we rarely, if ever, use this language today. When did you last hear a Christian friend's life described as "worthy of the gospel"? Chances are the answer is "not very often," and more likely "never." To "live worthy of the gospel of Christ" does not rank high on the priority lists of the twenty-first-century church. But Paul placed it high on his priority list. That is why he underlines it for the churches in Ephesus, Colossae, and Thessalonica, as well as Philippi.[1]

Why a Forgotten Calling?

So why has Paul's exhortation (and his way of thinking about the Christian life) dropped out of fashion when he obviously thought it was so important?

No doubt one reason is that we are (rightly) allergic to the idea that anyone could be worthy before God. We are all like the Roman centurion who said, "I am *not worthy* to have you come under my roof" (Luke 7:6), and like the prodigal son, who confessed, "I have sinned against heaven and before you. I am *no longer worthy* to be called your son" (Luke 15:21). And isn't Paul's whole point in Romans 1:18–3:20 to argue us into a corner, where we are forced to admit our unworthiness? Every mouth is shut in the presence of the holy God of heaven because we are all guilty,

---

1 Eph. 4:1; Phil. 1:27; Col. 1:10; 1 Thess. 2:12.

all unworthy (Rom. 3:19–20). We can only say with the dying Martin Luther: "We are beggars. This is true." Our hymnbooks (or overhead screens, for that matter) never teach us to sing, "I am worthy, I am worthy"—only "Thou art worthy, thou art worthy, O Lord."

So the gospel teaches us we are unworthy. We are saved by grace, not by worth.

Yet Paul prioritized our responsibility to live in a worthy manner. Why, then, are we reluctant to take his words at face value?

A Latent Fear of Legalism?

Another part of the answer is the fear we have that any exhortation to be worthy of the gospel is by definition legalism, or at least likely to lead to it. But if so, why did Paul, the apostle of grace, say this?

In recent years, grace has often been given a headline role in teaching and preaching, perhaps especially among younger evangelical preachers who have come to feel that too many Christians are prone to all kinds of legalism. There is too much of the atmosphere of "do" and "don't."

Certainly too many Christians have suffered from a "conditional" sense of acceptance with God—as though his love for us is ultimately dependent on how well we perform.

God then becomes like a schoolmaster to be pleased by a satisfactory performance, or a policeman who makes sure we are keeping the laws, whereas the gospel is about his grace, because it comes from "the God of all grace" (1 Pet. 5:10).

There is certainly something important in this emphasis. For since Eden we have all been legalists by nature. The assumption that somehow or another we have to do something to earn our way into God's favor is the default position of the human heart. That is why it is the characteristic most world religions have in common.

So the gospel tells us to bathe in God's grace.

But Paul well knew that *emphasizing* God's grace in Christ in reaction to legalism is not necessarily the same thing as *understanding* the grace of God in Christ.

Perhaps an illustration will make the point. I recall hearing a preacher expound a New Testament passage that emphasized the grace of God. But at the same time, the passage was punctuated by exhortations to holiness (as many passages are). During his exposition it became clear he thought at least some (and probably most!) of us listening to him still thought of God's grace as "conditional."

Maybe he was right. But instead of showing us how God's grace energizes us to obey God's commands and helping us to see the connections between God's grace and our response, he

4

simply ignored the exhortations. All he did was warn us against "legalism" without telling us how Christians who, like their Lord, want to live "by every word that comes from the mouth of God" (Matt. 4:4) can obey his commandments precisely *because of* God's grace. So his sermon missed teaching us this fundamental gospel principle: the richer and fuller the exposition of the grace of God in Christ, the safer it is to expound the all-demanding commands that flow from it as a result.

But this is what the New Testament teaches constantly. It is why Paul's letters are punctuated by words like *therefore* and *so*. For it is in the nature of God's grace that he gives all; but the grace that gives all also seeks all to be given in return; it can be satisfied with no less. Any young man or woman who has fallen in love knows this.

So to press the mute button on the commands of the New Testament actually subverts God's grace rather than highlighting it.

How Grace Relates to Obedience

The true relationship between grace and obedience is powerfully expressed in Paul's summary of the gospel in his letter to Titus:

> For the grace of God has appeared,
> bringing salvation for all people,

> training us to renounce ungodliness and worldly
>> passions,

and

> to live self-controlled, upright, and godly lives in
>> the present age,
> waiting for our blessed hope,
> the appearing of the glory of our great God and
>> Savior Jesus Christ,
> who gave himself for us
> to redeem us from all lawlessness

and

> to purify for himself a people for his own
>> possession
> who are zealous for good works.
>> (Titus 2:11–14 reformatted)

To which Paul adds a further exhortation to Titus himself:

> Declare these things; exhort and rebuke with all authority.
> Let no one disregard you. (Titus 2:15)

This is strong language—in its description of the wonder of grace, but also in the way it spells out its implications—not to mention what Titus is to do about it! The stronger the foundation of a house, the bigger and stronger the building itself can be. And the richer and fuller the exposition of God's grace, the more consuming the exhortations can be.

Geerhardus Vos once commented with great insight that the essence of legalism is to divorce the law of God from the person of God. It is "a peculiar kind of submission to law, something that no longer feels the personal divine touch in the rule it submits to."[2] So dividing the grace of God from his commandments becomes legalism. But separating God's commandments from his grace is not the solution. It only disguises the problem; it can never dissolve it. In fact, it turns both grace and law into impersonal realities in which we lose hold of God himself. No. The God of grace is also the God of commandments; the two belong together and need to be embraced together in Christ. To put it another way, knowing Christ as Savior and knowing him as Lord can never be separated; nor can justification and sanctification. They belong together in Christ. And as John Calvin shrewdly commented with some frequency, to isolate them from each other is to "tear Christ in pieces."[3]

---

2 Geerhardus Vos, *The Self-Disclosure of Jesus: The Modern Debate about the Messianic Consciousness*, ed. Johannes G. Vos (Nutley, NJ: Presbyterian and Reformed, 1953), 17.

3 For example, Calvin on 1 Cor. 1:30, in *Calvin's Commentaries*, vol. 20, trans. William Pringle (Grand Rapids, MI: Baker, 1996), 93.

The Meaning of "Worthy"

So what is implied in Paul's exhortation "Only let your manner of life be worthy [*axios*] of the gospel of Christ"?

In English versions of the New Testament, the Greek word *axios* is usually translated "worthy." But its flavor is expressed elsewhere when it is translated "in keeping with" (Matt. 3:8; Acts 26:20). Like many other words, there is a picture lying behind the origin of *axios*. It means "Properly, 'bringing up the other beam of the scales,' 'bringing into equilibrium,' and therefore 'equivalent.'"[4]

The basic idea is that a life that is worthy of the gospel of Christ expresses in the form of a lifestyle what the gospel teaches in the form of a message. Such a life takes on a character that reflects the character of the Lord Jesus Christ.

When I was a boy, my morning chore before school was to collect some of the provisions our family would need for the meals of the day. One of my tasks was to go to the local butcher. My mother charged me to ask for a specific cut of meat and a specific weight of it. In those now far-off days our butcher used old-fashioned scales with two pans. On

---

4 Werner Foerster, in Gerhard Kittel, *Theological Dictionary of the New Testament*, trans. and ed. G. W. Bromiley, vol. 1 (Grand Rapids: Eerdmans, 1964), 379.

one he placed weights to the amount I asked for. On the other he measured out the meat, adding to it or subtracting from it until the central pointer indicated a perfect balance between the two pans. It was fun to watch him add or subtract the meat in order to get just the right balance. Simple but ingenious!

That is the picture the word *axios* conveys. On the one hand, here is the gospel. And on the other hand, here is your life. And Paul's exhortation is this: Live in such a way that your life "weighs the same" as the gospel! Live in a way that is "in keeping with" the gospel, that "matches" the gospel. This is what "the balanced Christian life" looks like. The gospel is the message of the good news of Jesus Christ, and our lives are to be the embodiment of that good news. Put another way, the gospel is "the power of God for salvation" (Rom. 1:16), and we are to live in a powerfully saved way!

For Paul this was neither a trivial nor an optional matter. It was instead a "one and only" kind of thing, an essential.

A Kind of Citizenship

But "worthy" is not the only picture word Paul uses here. When he writes "*let your manner of life be* worthy of the gospel," he uses the Greek verb *politeuomai*. It is derived from the word for a city (*polis*, the source of our word *politics*). Literally it means "live as a citizen."

Paul could have used the verb meaning "walk," as he does in Ephesians ("walk in a manner worthy of the calling to which you have been called"—4:1) and Colossians ("walk in a manner worthy of the Lord"—1:10). But you can probably guess why he uses citizenship language. Philippi was a Roman colony; its civic life was structured according to Roman law and the Roman way of life. Citizens of Philippi were Roman citizens. That was why the local magistrates there had been so alarmed when they discovered that the man whose garments they had torn off and whom they had beaten with rods without due process of law and then thrown into prison—this man was in fact a Roman citizen. No wonder they came to Paul eating humble pie (Acts 16:22–23, 37–40).

Paul may simply have been saying in Philippians 1:27, "As citizens in Philippi live your life in a way that reflects the gospel." But there is almost certainly more. Was Lydia, who had first welcomed him, still there? The jailer and his family whom Paul had pointed to Christ surely were. And perhaps too the young slave girl Paul had rescued from abusive men and abusive spirits was listening. Paul was reminding them, "Our citizenship is in heaven" (3:20).

Philippi was not in Italy but in Macedonia. But a Philippian lived there as a citizen of Rome, according to Roman law, following the patterns of life in the capital city. Paul's message, then, was that while his friends were living in Philippi, their real citizenship was heavenly; their church family was a colony of heaven here on earth. And because that was true, they were to live not according to the pattern of life of any earthly city but according to the pattern of life of the heavenly city, the new Jerusalem.

In short, the Christian life is to be a version of "heaven on earth." The privilege could not be greater; and the standard could not be higher! For that reason, the summons could not be more demanding—nothing less than all-embracing. And yet, for all that, Paul's exhortation is a million miles from legalism *because he understands how the gospel works.*

The grace of God in Christ provides us with a new identity, a heavenly one; it follows that this—and not our natural identity—determines everything we do. Our identity, our citizenship, is heavenly. As Paul says elsewhere, our lives are "hidden with Christ in God" (Col. 3:3), and when Christ appears, to bring about our final transformation into his likeness, then our true identity will become clear (Phil. 3:20–21; Col. 3:4; 1 John 3:1–2). What, then, could be more logical, more compelling, than to live in this world as those who are citizens of another world? Like Daniel in the Old Testament, we are called to live out the lifestyle of the Jerusalem (above) to which we belong, even when we live in the Babylon (below) where we don't really belong.

So we are to "sing the LORD's song in a foreign land" (Ps. 137:4). That's not a matter of legalism, for "his commandments are not burdensome" (1 John 5:3). Jesus tells us that being yoked to him, the meek and lowly one, brings ease, not dis-ease, and rest, not restlessness, for our souls (Matt. 11:28–30).

I have lived in three different cities in the United States. At my regular visa interviews the consular official may ask me which of these cities I have enjoyed most (yes, I have been asked that question!). Presumably, she is thinking, "If he can answer that question in my presence, then he probably is the person his papers say he is, his fingerprints guarantee he is, and his passport photo seems to suggest he is." My answer is diplomatic. I mention things about each of the three cities I particularly appreciated. While inevitably there are similarities between them, each of them has its own distinctives. If someone asks us what life was like in city X, it is the distinctives we tend to mention—different atmospheres and styles of life, even peculiar ways people drive (!), as well as diverse accents and regional pronunciations. We tend to take on the lifestyles and even the speech styles of the places where we live.

A Curious Difference

As a Scot living in the United States, I used to enjoy riding the elevators ("lifts") in tall buildings, stopping floor by floor and occasionally exchanging comments with other passengers. Since my accent tended to betray me, sometimes as I left, someone would say, "And where are you *from*?" As I stepped out of the elevator and the doors began to close, I always enjoyed saying with a smile to the three or four people remaining on the elevator, "Columbia, South Carolina." The puzzled looks on their faces as the doors closed said: "You can't be from around here with an accent like that! Where are you *really from*?" Even if I lived there, it was obvious that I really "belonged" somewhere else.

That's the kind of thing Paul is talking about in Philippians 1:27. His Christian friends may have lived in the Roman colony of Philippi, but their real citizenship was in the kingdom of God; they should live that out—think "Sermon on the Mount" lifestyle. And if they did, people in Philippi would find themselves asking: "Where are you really from? There's something about you—I can't quite put my finger on it—but it's different. You're not really from around here."

I sometimes wondered what happened in the elevator after the doors closed. Did people say anything to each other? Did they try to work out where I was from? If I met them in the elevator again, would they remember me and ask: "Where are you *really* from? I love your accent—are you English?" (Help! But I have been introduced as "coming from Scotland, England"!)

That's a parable of what happened in the early church. And it contrasts with the church today. As a kind of tactic for witnessing, Christians today have often been encouraged to devise questions they can ask non-Christians. In this way perhaps a conversation about the gospel can be stimulated. It rarely strikes us how sharply this contrasts with the teaching of the New Testament. Simon Peter suggests that he expected the reverse would be the case: he expected that the quality of the lives of Christians would mean that non-Christians would be the ones asking the questions (1 Pet. 3:15): "What makes you tick?" "What is it about you? Why do you say these things and do these things?" "Tell me why you believe in God" "Who is Jesus Christ?" "Can I be forgiven?" "What does it mean to be a Christian?" Why the difference between today's evangelistic conversation starters and the questions Peter might have expected?

There is something here so obvious that we rarely notice it: the New Testament gives us virtually no advice about how to witness to Jesus Christ. Yet who can doubt the impact of the witness of the early church—all, apparently, without books, DVDs, TV programs, the Internet, or entire organizations and seminars led by experts. What explains the difference? Why in the West do we need to devise techniques for witnessing to Christ? Perhaps the simple answer is that we have not lived in a way that is worthy of the gospel of Christ. We have had all too little of the lifestyle, the atmosphere, or the accent of heaven, where Christ is.

C. S. Lewis has an insightful passage in which he comments on the laziness of some students who, instead of learning how to use a proof in geometry, learn it only by rote.[5] They don't realize that taking the easier way turns out to be the hard way and involves much more work, and in the end it doesn't work. Teachers sometimes observe this. I vividly remember the oral exam of a PhD candidate. He had already adequately completed sixteen hours of written questions in his preliminary written comprehensive exam. Yet he seemed incapable of responding to our questions. At the end of a repeat exam, a puzzled (and, like the rest

5   See C. S. Lewis, *Mere Christianity* (London: Fontana, 1955), 170–71.

of us, slightly exasperated) colleague said to him: "You did adequately on the written part; but you have done miserably in the oral part. How did you prepare for these exams?" His answer? "I memorized dictionary articles"—in fact, he had memorized around one hundred! I am sure others were thinking as I was, "It would have been easier if you had simply tried to *understand* the material!"

Living "worthy of the gospel of Christ" is not a matter of techniques. It involves the development of Christian character. It's about who and what we become in Christ. It is a slow, all-demanding, and arduous process. The easier and quicker option seems to be to learn how to get your life together and how to do things successfully. But to live worthy is much more a matter of living the life of the heavenly world while you are still here on earth; in the oft quoted and justly famous words of the Westminster Shorter Catechism, it means to become someone who knows what it means "to glorify God, and to enjoy him for ever."[6]

B. B. Warfield,[7] probably the most significant American evangelical theologian of the past century, illustrates this point with a wonderful story:

---

6 Answer 1.

7 Benjamin B. Warfield (1851–1921) was longtime professor of systematic theology at Princeton Theological Seminary. Among other things, he was a distant

We have the following bit of personal experience from a general officer of the United States army. He was in a great western city at a time of intense excitement and violent rioting. The streets were over-run daily by a dangerous crowd. One day he observed approaching him a man of singularly combined calmness and firmness of mien, whose very demeanor inspired confidence. So impressed was he with his bearing amid the surrounding uproar that when he had passed he turned to look back at him, only to find that the stranger had done the same. On observing his turning the stranger at once came back to him, and touching his chest with his forefinger, demanded without preface: "What is the chief end of man?" On receiving the countersign, "Man's chief end is to glorify God and to enjoy him forever" — "Ah!" said he, "I knew you were a Shorter Catechism boy by your looks!" "Why, that was just what I was thinking of you," was the rejoinder.

It is worthwhile to be a Shorter Catechism boy. They grow to be men. And better than that, they are exceedingly apt to grow to be men of God.[8]

---

relative of Wallis Warfield Simpson, the femme fatale in the abdication of the British monarch Edward VIII.

8   B. B. Warfield, "Is the Shorter Catechism Worthwhile?," in *Selected Shorter Writings of Benjamin B. Warfield*, ed. John E. Meeter, vol. 1 (Nutley, NJ: Presbyterian and Reformed, 1970), 383–84.

The ultimate point, of course, is not merely learning the Shorter Catechism—valuable though that may be. It is learning how the gospel of Jesus Christ transforms our character and builds Christlikeness into it—a Christlikeness that cannot be hidden and makes its own impression on others. For becoming "worthy of the gospel of Christ" is, in simple terms, becoming more like the Lord Jesus.

2

To Be Worthy

Some Basic Grammar

"SELF-HELP" BOOKS HAVE HAD phenomenal success in recent decades. In the past the "how to" literary genre tended to be confined to manuals for do-it-yourself enthusiasts. A few bestsellers were of the "self-help, life improvement" variety—like Dale Carnegie's famous *How to Make Friends and Influence People.* But now such titles abound, and they have their own incarnation in the books Christians read. We want to know "how to be a Christian."

The titles are usually more subtle than that. But it would surely not surprise us to learn that so many contemporary Christian books belong to the "how to" variety. Scan the lists of Christian bestsellers, and they are likely to be heavy with books about ourselves, our potentials and how to fulfill them, or our problems and how to solve them. They are less likely to be about God and what he has done for us in Christ, or about Christian character. They are heavier on how to be *doing*, lighter on *being*, and lightest on *the ultimate Being*.

A subset of "how to" books is increasingly popular with pastors and preachers. These explain "how to teach/preach [Bible book A or B]" and so forth. Busy pastors no longer have time to wade through major commentaries, read books on Christology, wrestle with the doctrine of the Trinity, or reflect on the meaning of the image of God. People need their problems solved, not their heads stuffed. And preaching must address the issues of the day. Or so it seems.

Some time ago, a younger minister told me that a senior minister had asked him if he had ever read a book on the Trinity. "Three cheers for that senior minister," you might think. But no. The younger minister quietly responded that he had (you would think any preacher worth his salt would have read books on the Trinity!). The *senior minister* then told him that he had just finished reading the first book he had ever read on the Trinity. (What was he thinking about when he baptized people?)

This is symptomatic of our spiritual condition. It is easy to lament this situation, and it is lamentable. But it is just here that some of us (at least) need to be careful. Yes, focusing on the "how to" without knowing the "what is" turns the gospel on its head. But equally, focusing on "what is" without asking "how to" tends to inflate heads without nourishing lives. It truncates the gospel. We need to ask the "how to" questions simply because the New Testament makes us ask them—and helps us to answer them too.

This is true; but it is not always obvious.

Have you sometimes felt slightly frustrated when Paul tells you *what* you are to become but doesn't seem to tell you *how* you can do it? Perhaps that explains why so many Christians turn to books, or seminars, or teachers who specialize in the "how to." In fact what appeals to us about them is probably that (1) they are talking about *us*, and (2) their teaching is very "practical."

But the Scriptures also talk about us. And surely no right-thinking Christian is going to say that the Bible isn't a practical book. Perhaps therefore the problem is that we haven't been reading it properly; we haven't listened carefully enough. Indeed, perhaps if we reflected on a passage of Scripture a little more patiently, we might discover that embedded in its teaching of "what is" is also its teaching on "how to."

If we are to do that, we first need to learn the language the gospel speaks. And in particular, we need to understand that the gospel of Jesus Christ has its own grammar. If our own lives are going to be worthy of Christ, we need to learn it.

The Grammar of the Gospel

Most of us pick up the grammatical rules of our own language unconsciously. In some ways it is a pity we call them "rules," but rules help us communicate and play fair. A game of rugby is played according to its rules (and woe betide any American who, invited to play, picks up the ball and throws it forward, unless it's a "throw in," since rugby involves moving the ball forward while always throwing it backward!). The rules are what make it possible to play the game.

Languages work in the same way. We pick up the rules of our own "language game" as we play. And we rarely give much thought to them until a language pedant tells us when it should be "William and I" and when it should be "William and me."

The big challenge in learning a foreign language is not only the different accents people have, or even the different alphabets they use when they write, but also that words are spelled differently, and there are different rules of grammar. It can all seem impossibly difficult, because it is so counter-cultural to us.

One of my childhood memories from elementary school is having a disagreement with a teacher. That in itself was remarkable, because we rarely spoke in class except when we shouldn't! But my teacher had written on the blackboard (yes, blackboard!) the word *height*. I remember putting my hand up and saying: "Miss, that's the wrong spelling. It should be *h-i-g-h-t*. We spell *high h-i-g-h*, so it should be *h-i-g-h-t*"!

I cringe at the memory. I was obviously a stubborn stickler for letter logic! But that was the day I discovered that English isn't logical—at least it didn't fit into my seven-year-old logic.

The gospel is like that. It has its own logic, which is expressed in its own grammar. And it is spoken with an accent all its own.

Before we become Christians, this new language seems to defy our logic. Think of how Jesus said to Nicodemus that it was impossible for a person to *see* the kingdom of God unless he or she was "born again." Nicodemus—"the teacher of Israel" (John 3:10)—replied, in essence, "Jesus, I just can't *see* that!" Jesus told him that without the new birth a person can never see the kingdom, and Nicodemus suggested that can't be right. Why? Because he couldn't see it! He didn't understand this new language and essentially told the Master, "Look, Jesus, a man can't get back into his mother's womb and begin again, can he?"

The gospel has a grammar of its own. Paul reminds us that we are to live as "citizens" of a different country, and that means we speak a different language.

What are the "rules" that govern this new language of the gospel? We learn them naturally by listening to and observing more mature Christians—that is part of the beauty of the church family. But it helps to focus on the most basic elements of the grammar of the gospel. Here are some of them.

Moods

We have moods, and verbs also have moods! But when we are talking about grammar, *mood* is really a variation of *mode*—how a verb works. For our purposes, the two most important moods are (1) the indicative mood, where the verb expresses a fact, and (2) the imperative mood, where the verb issues a command.

Now, with this in mind, think about Jesus's conversation with Nicodemus again. Jesus states a fact: to see and enter the kingdom of God it is necessary to be born again. Nicodemus essentially asks in return, "How can anyone do this?" He assumes that the way to be accepted in God's kingdom is by what we do, confusing imperative with indicative.

Don't most people you know think that way? They think that the way to be accepted by God is to do the best you can, and God will accept you. Sure, you might not be perfect, but heaven helps those who help themselves. So long as you do your best—and can safely assume that's as good as the next person—you'll pass.

Putting that in grammatical terms, the instinctive rule people follow is this:

The *imperative*, "Do your best,"

leads to

the *indicative*, "If you do that, then God will save you."

But the gospel uses a different grammar; its rule is this:

The *indicative*, "Christ died for our sins" (1 Cor. 15:3),

leads to

the *imperative*, "Believe in the Lord Jesus, and you will be saved" (Acts 16:31).

Or again,

the *indicative*, "In Christ God was reconciling the world to himself" (2 Cor. 5:19), leads to

the *imperative*, "Be reconciled to God" (2 Cor. 5:20).

The indicative and imperative belong together—the one leads to the other—but we mangle the gospel if we confuse the order. Even if an imperative precedes the indicative in the order of a sentence, in the order of the logic of the grammar of the gospel, God's indicatives are always the foundation for his imperatives. God's grace is always the ground and motive for our obedience—never the other way around.

The Bible is full of examples of this. From the very beginning, in Genesis 2,

the indicative (grace), "You may surely eat of every tree of the garden" (v. 16),

leads to

the imperative (obedience), "Of the tree of the knowledge of good and evil you shall not eat" (v. 17).

And just as important for us to notice is the same logic in the giving of God's Ten Commandments in Exodus 20:

The indicative, "I am the LORD . . . who brought you out of the land of Egypt, out of the house of slavery" (v. 2),

leads to

the imperative, "You shall have no other gods before me" (v. 3).

By the time Paul was writing to the Philippians he had been using the grammar of the gospel for years. It had become second nature to him. But he could look back on earlier days when he had used a different language grammar altogether. At that time, he had believed he possessed "a righteousness of my own that comes from the law" and was "blameless" (Phil. 3:6, 9). His former language essentially worked like this:

The imperative, "Keep the commandments,"

should lead to

the indicative, "As a result you will be blameless before God."

But then he met Christ, began to understand the gospel, learned its language fluently, and discovered the opposite:

The indicative, "Righteousness before God comes through Christ,"

leads to

the imperative, "Trust in Jesus Christ alone for righteousness, and then you will have a righteousness from God."

Why belabor this point? Because we tend to forget it or reverse it—*and not only before we become Christians but afterward as well.* This rule of gospel grammar is unvarying from the beginning of the Christian life to its end: God's indicatives are the foundation for all of his imperatives; his resources are the source of our transformation. We are never thrown back on our own resources but are always invited into his.

So, when we read Paul's *imperative* "Let your manner of life be worthy of the gospel of Christ," we must ask, "On what *indicative of God's grace* does this imperative rest?" For this is an overwhelming imperative. It could crush us, and on its own it will. So, what sustains it?

Yes, it is right to ask, "How can I do this?" But we must first ask, "What does *God* do to make this possible?" and we must absorb his resources. A major part of the answer to this question lies in understanding another feature of the grammar of the gospel: prepositions.

Prepositions

Prepositions relate things to each other in different ways. You may tell a friend, "I have to run an errand *before* our meeting, but we can talk *after* lunch." The words "before" and "after" are prepositions of time. If you tell your friend you will meet her "*outside* the restaurant," you have used a preposition of place.

The most important preposition in Christian vocabulary is a preposition of place: *in*. And its most significant use is the expression "in Christ." Paul uses it more than eighty times, not counting similar expressions like "in him" or "in whom." In addition, he uses the expression "in the Lord" more than forty times.

It may come as a surprise to us that there is no evidence Paul ever used the word *Christian*. In fact, we know of only one occasion when we can be sure he even heard the word— and then it was used disparagingly![1] The way Paul thought about himself was as "a man in Christ."

I remember, as a youngster, puzzling over Paul's words in 2 Corinthians 12:2: "I know a man in Christ who fourteen

1   By King Agrippa in Acts 26:28.

years ago was caught up to the third heaven." Who was this man Paul knew? Only later did it dawn on me that he was talking about himself! *He* was that "man in Christ." This was his most basic way of describing what it meant for him to be a Christian—someone who was united to Christ, so that all that Christ had done for him became his. To become a Christian means no longer to be "in Adam." Says Paul, "If anyone is in Christ, he or she has entered into a new creation; the old is gone, the new has come" (2 Cor. 5:17 AT). This is why Paul says in Ephesians 1:3–14 that those who are in Christ have come to enjoy every spiritual blessing in him.

Paul expounds this in great detail in two passages: Romans 6:1–14 and Colossians 3:1–17. Together they give us a breathtaking picture of what it means to belong to Christ and to be "in" him.

We can do no more than summarize here: the believer is someone who, through his or her faith union with the Lord Jesus, has died to the dominion or lordship of sin and been raised to new life. More than that, our true life is now hidden with Christ in God. In fact, Paul says, we are so profoundly united to Christ that not even death will destroy our union with him, and when he appears, we shall appear in glory with him.

In Romans 6:1–14—one of the most important passages in the New Testament—Paul makes clear that fundamental to a life worthy of the gospel is knowing who we are in Christ. In these verses he indicates that we belong to a new category of individuals who share a common characteristic: we are defined by the fact that we have died to sin and been raised into newness of life. When he asks in verse 2, "How can *we who died to sin* still live in it?" he uses a form of the personal pronoun that implies belonging to a category or group—the category of those who have died to sin and been raised into new life. This is what now defines us. This is who we are. It is our new identity now because—as he has just explained in Romans 5:12–21—we are no longer "in Adam" but "in Christ."

If we are in Christ, then here is the truth about us: We are no longer under the dominion of sin. We have been set free from it in Christ.

> The death he [Christ] died he died to sin, once for all, but the life he lives he lives to God. So you also must consider yourselves dead to sin and alive to God in Christ Jesus.
>
> Let not sin therefore reign in your mortal body, to make you obey its passions. (Rom. 6:10–12)

This, then, is *who we are; it is our identity.* To fail to think this way about myself is to suffer from a loss of my spiritual identity. No wonder, then, if I fail to live a life worthy of the gospel of Jesus Christ, I have had a truncated understanding of what that gospel has accomplished!

This second rule of grammar leads us to a third that is related to it.

Tenses

When we speak or write, we use tenses, the most basic ones being past, present, and future. The gospel teaches us that, as Christians, we are to live in the present. But it also teaches us to do that conscious of the fact that in Christ we live in light of both the past and the future, or as we sometimes say, the "already" and the "not yet."

In his death, resurrection, and ascension, the Lord Jesus has *already* done everything we need for salvation. But he has *not yet* brought his work to its consummation. That still awaits his second coming. Because we are "in Christ," we have *already* died to sin and are no longer under its reign (Rom. 6:14). But sin has *not yet* died in us. And until it does, we will have to fight against it all our lives. The marvelous truth is that the most important thing has *already* been accomplished—sin's reign over us has *already* been brought to an end. That is why it is possible for us to resist its influence over us even though it has *not yet* been destroyed in us!

Think of it this way. I have British friends who have become American citizens. If the British government wrote to them saying they now had to do military service, they could write back and say: "You know, there is still part of me that makes me feel I should do that. But you are no longer my master! I am not under your authority. I have been set free from it."

It is the same with the reign of sin.

This has further profound implications for the way our lives express the grammar of the gospel. And this brings us to another element in it.

Negatives and Positives

Statements in general and commands (imperatives) in particular are either positive (do this) or negative (don't do this).

The gospel is full of rich and wonderful positives—in Christ we have been raised into new life and been blessed with every spiritual blessing (Eph. 1:3–14). But those positives also require us to introduce negatives into our lives.

Today negatives are out of fashion. In virtually every sphere of life we are being urged to get rid of "negativity." The only thing to be negative about is . . . being negative!

But it is not so in the Christian life, because the deep logic of the gospel leads to both positive and negative implications.

Take the Philippians, who were being urged to live worthy of the gospel. They were citizens of heaven because they were "in Christ Jesus" (Phil. 1:1). They possessed a new identity because they were now citizens in the kingdom of those who have died to the dominion of sin and been raised up into newness of life.

But, at the same time, they were also "at Philippi." They were living out the new life in the old world. In addition, they were not yet living the new life in resurrection bodies. So long as that was true, the Philippians would need "negativity"—for example, they were to be negative about "grumbling or disputing" (Phil. 2:14) and about "confidence in the flesh" (Phil. 3:3) or thinking they had arrived spiritually (Phil. 3:12). And they were also to be profoundly negative about the influence of people who were "enemies of the cross of Christ" (Phil. 3:18).

So Paul was urging the Philippian Christians positively to live as citizens of heaven; but this implied, negatively, that they were not to live as though they belonged to Philippi. He puts essentially the same idea in his famous words to the Romans: "*Do not be conformed* to this world, *but be transformed* by the renewal of your mind" (Rom. 12:2). And, of course, these negative and positive imperatives were rooted in this glorious indicative: "I appeal to you therefore, brothers, by the mercy of God." They were to think about who they were now—younger brothers (and sisters) and joint heirs with Christ—because they had received the mercy of God.

There are depths to this pattern to which we will need to return. But for the moment, we should notice the rhythm of life that is expressed in these words. The person whose life is worthy of the gospel walks spiritually with both feet in a balanced way: a *negative* step (*Do not be* conformed . . .) and a *positive* step (*Do be* transformed . . .). Just as there is always an indicative and an imperative in the grammar of the gospel, there will always be a positive-and-negative rhythm, a yes and a no.

Thus the life that is worthy of the gospel of Christ is a daily outworking of Titus 2:11–13:

Indicative: "The grace of God has appeared, bringing salvation . . ."

Imperative: "training us to"

Negative: "renounce ungodliness and worldly passions"

Positive: "and to live self-controlled, upright, and godly lives in this present age, waiting for our blessed hope, the appearing of the glory of our great God and Savior Jesus Christ."

And while we are thinking about these verses, notice the *already* and the *not yet*:

Already: The grace has already appeared, and we are living in the new "present age."

Not yet: We are "waiting for . . . the appearing of . . . Jesus Christ."

As we begin to notice this pattern repeatedly in the Bible, we gradually learn to speak the language of grace with some degree of fluency. Its grammar becomes increasingly instinctive. We dig down deep into the great indicative foundations of the gospel so that we can respond to the all-consuming imperatives of grace. As we do this, we appreciate increasingly what it means to be "in Christ" while we are still in this world; we therefore walk steadily on both feet, as it were, rejoicing in what Christ has already accomplished both *for* us and *in* us (more prepositions to understand and learn to use). And we realize that the work he has *already* begun in us is *not yet* complete—and seeing this we begin to understand why we need to develop this built-in rhythm of negative responses to sin and positive developments of grace.

A Way of Walking

Our family is Scottish, and (for some, at least) part of the definition of being Scottish is playing golf (and thankfully Scotland is still a country where almost everywhere a person of modest means can afford to be a member of the local golf club).

I remember one summer evening going to our golf club to collect two of our boys at the end of their round. It was before the days when everyone carried a cell phone, and I did not know that they were so enjoying themselves that they decided to play some more holes. As I waited, the sun began to go down. And then, on the horizon, I saw two silhouettes appearing. There was a seven-year gap between the boys, and at that time one was much taller than the other. They walked slowly from the seventeenth green to the eighteenth tee, the younger and shorter boy following his elder brother. As they did so, I found myself experiencing a special emotion. "These are my sons," I thought, "I would recognize their walk anywhere. It moves me deeply and draws out my affection to see the younger brother following his older brother!"

Something similar is true of us as Christians. The gospel calls us to a style of walking that is recognizable anywhere.

The special affection I felt for my sons that evening prompted thoughts about another affection: What if our heavenly Father feels the same about us as he works out his purpose in us so that we might "be conformed to the image of his Son, in order that he might be the firstborn among many brothers" (Rom. 8:29)? Does he too say quietly to himself, moved with affection for us: "These are my sons, and I would recognize their walk anywhere; it moves me deeply and draws out my affection for them to see these younger brothers following their older brother the Lord Jesus"?

If that is true—and surely it is—isn't that a sufficiently powerful indicative of grace to help you respond to the imperatives of loving obedience?

3

Being Made Worthy

God's Instruments to Change Us

BEFORE WE COME TO FAITH IN CHRIST, the gospel is, by and large, a foreign language to us. And even after we become Christians, learning it takes some major adjustments.

Learning a New Language

Some foreign languages have connections to our own: they may have a common source; they may use the same alphabet. But other languages strike us at first as being impossible to learn. They involve too many major adjustments.

Take Hebrew, for example. Some of my books have been translated into Hebrew. But if I gave you a copy, the first thing you might notice would be that the alphabet is entirely different. And then, chances are you would mistake the back of the book for the front, and you might even hold it upside down! Why? Because the "back" of the book is the front! That doesn't make sense—until you remember that you read Hebrew from the right-hand side of the page to the left. That's why it makes perfect logical sense for the front of the book to be at the "back."

Confused? There's more. If I gave you my copy of the Hebrew Bible, you would notice some strange-looking marks *underneath* the words. These are called "vowel points." But if I now gave you one of my own books translated into modern Hebrew, you'd notice that those vowel points have vanished! Native Hebrew speakers know what the words mean without the help of vowels. It takes a little getting used to. But if I wrote, "Th_ c_t s_t _n th_ m_t," you wouldn't have too much difficulty knowing it was "the cat sat on the mat."

But at first, learning Hebrew is a struggle for most people. A new alphabet! Unfamiliar words for the same things! Different sounds from the ones you usually make! Opening the book at the back! Reading the words backward! Strange squiggles underneath the words! Then words with no vowels! How can anyone learn this language? Yet people do. Probably your minister once learned Hebrew, and perhaps even came to love its orderly beauty!

Learning a language that is in a different language family from our own—like Hebrew—is a process. A kind of deconstruction of how English works has to take place at the same time a reconstruction is gradually built up in our minds as to how Hebrew works.

The Pattern of Death and Resurrection

Something similar has to happen to us if we are to learn to speak the language of the gospel and are to become "worthy of the gospel of Christ." Paul puts it very vividly when he says that in getting to know Christ, he wants to "know . . . the power of his resurrection, and . . . share his sufferings, becoming like him in his death, that by any means possible I may attain to the resurrection from the dead" (Phil. 3:10–11).

Paul regularly speaks about this pattern of death and resurrection. It is as if the lenses in the eyeglasses through which he viewed his life were ground to a prescription that provided a new kind of twenty-twenty vision. He now viewed everything in his life in terms of his union with the crucified and risen Christ, creating a pattern of death and life, or of deconstruction and reconstruction.

Later writers have seen the same pattern embedded in Scripture. You do not need to have studied Latin to guess what John Calvin meant when he called it *mortificatio et vivificatio* and recognized that Scripture teaches that these are both *interna et externa*.[1]

What does this mean? If we are "in Christ," we are united to Christ in his death to sin and his resurrection to new life. This then works its way out in the whole of our lives in the way we put sin to death and put on Christ (Col. 3:1–4, 5, 12).

It also works out in the external as well as the internal aspects of our lives. So Paul could also speak in vivid terms about

> always carrying in the body the death of Jesus, so that the life of Jesus may also be manifested in our bodies. For we who live are always being given over to death for Jesus' sake, so that the life of Jesus may also be manifested in our mortal flesh. (2 Cor. 4:10–12).

Paul seems to have felt that God made him a kind of large-scale working model of how the gospel embeds deep patterns into our lives. When we read about his life, we can see on a large screen, as it were, the pattern that is being worked out usually on a much smaller scale in our own lives. Since union

---

1 Mortification and vivification are both internal and external.

with Christ in his death and resurrection lies at the foundation of the Christian life, from beginning to end it will involve deconstruction and reconstruction.

There remains etched in my memory the very number of the room in my university residence where I first read Martin Luther's preface to Romans. He wrote:

> The sum and substance of this letter is: to pull down, to pluck up, and to destroy all wisdom and righteousness of the flesh. . . .
>
> As Christ says through the prophet Jeremiah: "to pluck up and to break down and to destroy and to overthrow" (Jer. 1:10), namely, everything that is in us (i.e., all that pleases us because it comes from ourselves and belongs to us) and "to build and to plant," namely, everything that is outside of us and in Christ.[2]

This is how the gospel works—by demolition and reconstruction. God does this partly through his gracious watchcare over our lives as he shapes our character through his sovereign and wise and sometimes painful providence. Other

---

2 *Luther: Lectures on Romans*, trans. and ed. Wilhelm Pauck, Library of Christian Classics (London: SCM, 1961), 3–4.

elements of it lie in the way we seek to "put to death . . . what is earthly" and "put on" the graces of Christ (Col. 3:5, 12). This is a standing principle.

Martin Luther was applying words God had spoken originally to Jeremiah to illustrate how the gospel works: it comes

> to pluck up and to break down,
> to destroy and to overthrow,
> to build and to plant. (Jer. 1:10)

Four centuries later, in his book *Mere Christianity*, C. S. Lewis similarly made imaginative use of a building metaphor:

> Imagine yourself as a living house. God comes in to rebuild that house. At first, perhaps, you understand what He is doing. He is getting the drains right and stopping the leaks in the roof and so on: you knew that those jobs needed doing and so you are not surprised. But presently he starts knocking the house about in a way that hurts abominably and does not seem to make sense. What on earth is He up to? The explanation is that He is building quite a different house from the one you thought of—throwing out a wing here, putting on an extra floor there, running up towers, making courtyards. You thought you were going

to be made into a decent little cottage: but He is building a palace. He intends to come and live in it Himself.[3]

Deconstruction and reconstruction—this is the divine pattern of transformation. Because our lives, thoughts, motives, desires, and behavior patterns have been deeply complicated by sin, his untangling them, detoxifying us, and making us "worthy" can seem a long and sometimes painful process. But the goal is essentially a simple one. Our heavenly Father intends to make us like his incarnate Son, transforming us into his likeness. God's simple "purpose" is that we should be "conformed to the image of his Son, in order that he might be the firstborn among many brothers" (Rom. 8:28–29). That is what it means to be "worthy of the gospel of Christ."

God is engaged in art restoration of the most challenging kind. He restores lives in which his image and likeness have been defaced by sin and well-nigh destroyed. He will not be content with a "touch up job" but intends a complete restoration. And in this process, he will patiently clear away multiple layers of dirt that have spoiled his original work of art. He will restore the original color and repair the damage

3   C. S. Lewis, *Mere Christianity* (London: Fontana, 1955), 170–71.

to the very canvas of our lives. And then he will add the final glaze of glorification. In this process, he employs, by his Spirit, all the resources he has stored up in Christ to make us "worthy." But the restoration of the *worthy* always means that the *unworthy* will need to be removed.

This pattern emerges very clearly in the New Testament. Paul himself was a grand-scale working model of it. But the divine design runs through the whole Bible. Other individuals' lives also read like "large print" versions of the pattern. They enable us to read the miniature versions of it in our own lives. But miniature though they may be, with biblical lenses in our eyeglasses the pattern is still clear enough for us to read.

The familiar and much-loved story of Joseph is a classic, big-print version of the pattern.[4]

The Multicolored Life of Joseph

Picture the scene. Seventeen-year-old, good-looking Joseph ben Jacob sits down for breakfast with his family. He is wearing the "robe of many colors" his father had arranged to have specially made for him because he "loved Joseph more than any other of his sons" (foolish man!). Jacob's lack of wisdom

---

4 Gen. 37–50.

is repeated in his son, who, as Scottish people would say, has already "clyped" on his brothers—he has "brought a bad report of them to their father." Not surprisingly, they "hated him and could not speak peacefully to him" (Gen. 37:1–4).

Instead of treading carefully on the eggshells at breakfast, Joseph unwisely and insensitively blurts out, in effect, "Listen up everybody, I had a dream last night: we were all out in the fields at harvest, binding the sheaves—and *your* sheaves all came and bowed down to *my* sheaf!"

Not content with the irritation he has caused, and perhaps so wrapped up in himself that he does not even notice the hurt he has already brought or the further damage he is now doing, Joseph appears another morning at the breakfast table and recounts a second dream. This time the players are celestial, not terrestrial: "Behold, the sun, the moon, and eleven stars were bowing down to me" (Gen. 37:9). Mercifully, his mother's comments are not recorded! I know what my mother would have said: "To think that a son of mine could be so stupid!"

Of course what makes the rest of the story so gripping is the way these dreams become reality. But what makes it so *instructive* is how this happens and what it leads to.

By the end of the story at least three major reversals have taken place:

1. Father Jacob has a changed attitude toward all his sons.
2. The brothers have a changed attitude both toward their father and toward Joseph.
3. Joseph has become everything that he was not when he blurted out his dreams—namely, humble, wise, patient, and caring.

In terms of our theme, we might say that Prime Minister Joseph has at last been made "worthy" of the dreams he experienced as a seventeen-year-old. Then he lacked the patience needed to let his dream unfold on its own without anyone knowing of it. He was lacking in sensitivity and wisdom. Instead of keeping his mouth shut, he insisted on talking. He cared more about himself and his dreams than about his family. But all that was to be transformed.

What is remarkable is that in large measure the whole story depends on these failings of Joseph—but only because God graciously, sovereignly, wisely, and providentially works for Joseph's good, deconstructing him and then transforming him.

Genesis uses a recurring expression that explains how it all happens: "The LORD was with Joseph" (39:2, 21, 23). And so, by the end of the story he has become a man recognized for his divinely gifted wisdom, and he shows the most amazing patience both in the way he handles the years of plenty and of famine and, even more, in the way he handles his family. When his brothers visit Egypt in the years of famine and fail to realize that the prime minister with whom they must deal is actually their brother, there is no immediate blurting out of his identity on Joseph's part. There is no "It's me, Joseph! I told you so!" as they bow down before him. There is only a patient, wise, caring dealing with them that, in its own way, leads to their transformation and ultimately to the restoration of family fellowship.

Great narratives often share a similar structure. The storyline moves in a downward spiral until it reaches its nadir. Then comes a turning point, and it then moves upward to its triumphant conclusion. As the story unfolds, the author plants in it details and clues that make sense only when events have unfolded to their denouement.

So it is here.

In Joseph's story, there are two significant indications of the passage of time. When we first meet him, he is seventeen years old (Gen. 37:2). He is characterized by a lack of wisdom, care, and patience in equal measures. He is self-centered rather than God-centered.

The years that follow constitute a downward spiral in his life, until we find him falsely accused of attempted rape and languishing in prison as the forgotten interpreter of dreams.

But then the turning point comes when he is asked to interpret Pharaoh's dreams, and his Spirit-given wisdom is recognized by his appointment as prime minister of Egypt.

Just at this point the narrator slips into the story the words "Joseph was thirty years old when he entered the service of Pharaoh king of Egypt" (Gen. 41:46). By the Bible's inclusive mode of reckoning, fourteen years have passed since we first met him. The narrator is telling us something here. For fourteen years God has been with Joseph, despite himself, to prepare him for—yes—the fourteen years that will follow, seven of plenty and then seven of famine.

The slow and at times painful deconstruction has included a remarkable reconstruction.

Joseph is now in *the place* God intended him to be, at *the time* God planned. The important thing to him is the hand of God on his life. Remember his words when he revealed himself to his brothers? "I am your brother, Joseph, whom you sold into Egypt. . . . God sent me before you to preserve life. . . . God sent me before you to preserve for you a remnant on earth. . . . So it was not you who sent me here, but God" (Gen. 45:4–8).

But most important of all, through these years of divine deconstruction and reconstruction, God has made him *the man* for that place and time. God was preparing him for his great work—not only to "preserve" or save the lives of many (Gen. 45:5, 7; 50:20) but also to bring about reconciliation in his family. He is now wise, patient, caring, and God-centered!

Deconstruction and reconstruction, demolition and restoration, pulling up the weeds and planting the good seed. It is as though echoes of death and resurrection are heard not only after Christ had finished his work—in Paul, for example—but even prior to it, in people like Joseph. Of course! For just as we today are united to the Christ who has already come and share in the outworking of his death and resurrection, so too Old Testament believers were united by faith to the Christ who was promised.

Thus the ultimate blueprint revealed in Christ is expressed already in Joseph as it is in all of the Lord's people in every age. We see it repeatedly in the Scriptures, and then throughout the history of the church until we see it once again employed in the shaping and molding of our own lives too.

God is not malicious. But he takes his purpose seriously. And he takes our desire to be "worthy" seriously too. The priceless work of divine artistry in which he expressed his likeness in human form in us has been stolen. But now his Son has recovered it from the thief. Now God is beginning the painstaking work of restoration, removing the dirt, working on the canvas, restoring the original likeness in all its rich color. He means to put his skill on display to the angels and to point to his people and essentially say, "See my handiwork!" (see Eph. 3:10).

If paintings could feel and speak, they might tell us that art restoration is a very sore process! But to see the admiration on the faces of those who gaze on the finished product is worth all the pain.

So it is for the Christian.

But how does God engage in this work with its removal of the dirt, its scraping away of the layers of overpainting, and its repair of the canvas? How does he restore and then enhance the original? Basically in two ways: one is by the hand of his providence, and the other is by the word of his mouth.

The Hand of Providence

God employs friction to shape us into his Son's likeness. Scripture reflects on this in various places. One that provides us with important first principles is Romans 5:3–4: "We rejoice in our sufferings, knowing that suffering produces endurance, and endurance produces character, and character produces hope."

Paul has been explaining how knowing we are justified leads to rejoicing in the hope, or assurance, of the glory of

God. Christ was "delivered up for our trespasses and raised for our justification" (Rom. 4:25).

In his resurrection, our sin bearer, the Lord Jesus, was declared to be "righteous" in God's sight. When we are united to Christ, God declares us to be righteous in his sight too. And because our justification is actually Christ's justification for us, we can rejoice in the hope of glory.

In Romans, Paul takes several chapters to show that we cannot be justified by our own righteousness. Likewise, he tells the Philippians that only when we abandon our efforts to attain our own righteousness by observing the law, and instead trust in Christ, can we begin to enjoy the righteousness that comes from God (Phil. 3:9). And because that righteousness is ours in Christ, we know that it is as irreversible as his resurrection, and as perfect and complete as his! Think of it: you can never be more justified than you were the moment you trusted Christ! The greatest saint is no more justified than the newest believer! That justification is sure; it is perfect; it is irreversible; it is therefore final. It is guaranteed!

No wonder, then, if we rejoice or boast and exult in the assurance we have of the glory of God (Rom. 5:2). But Paul says there is more. More than rejoicing in the hope of glory? Can anything be more remarkable than that?

Think of it this way. It is *understandable* that if you have that kind of assurance, you will rejoice. But it is *remarkable* that you will rejoice *in your sufferings*. And *that* is what Paul goes on to say.

Paul was not a masochist. He didn't perversely enjoy pain. But notice that it isn't the pain that causes his rejoicing. It is the *productivity* of the pain—the fact that "suffering *produces* endurance" (Rom. 5:3). Then endurance "*produces* character [that is, tested or proven character]" (Rom. 5:4). And this in turn leads us again to the hope or assurance of God's glory—but this time the glory we hope for will be *in us* as well as *for us*.

The word "endurance" (ESV) translates the Greek word *hypomonē*. Its basic idea is being able to remain, to keep standing, under something.

Think of Olympic weight lifters, their whole bodies shuddering under the enormous weights placed on the barbells they lift. It isn't eating a particular breakfast cereal that enables them to remain standing under the weight. They can do that only because over the weeks, months, and even years they have been in the gym. Their strength is developed through pressure. So it is with us: strength, endurance, stickability, being able to keep going—that kind of "tried and tested character" is developed only through pressure.

Paul's word translated "character" (*dokimē*) really means "the quality of having been tested and approved." This is what puts character, substance, strength, reliability, trustworthiness, and dependability into our lives. Character doesn't just appear out of nowhere; it is the result of God's refining our lives through tribulation—and, yes, even suffering.

When I was a small boy, my mother used to get me to help her clean and polish everything in the house made of brass—from candlesticks to door plates and doorknobs. She would apply multipurpose liquid polish to each surface and leave it to dry, and then we would return to rub each item vigorously with a soft cloth. My mother's test of success was for us to squat down together at the doorknobs to see our faces reflected in them.

The memory remains with me as an illustration of the way God uses pressure and friction in our lives. He is "polishing" our graces until he can see his image reflected in us. That's how he makes us "worthy" by his hand operating in providence. The relation between suffering and glory, then, is not only chronological (suffering now, glory then); it is also causal: "We suffer with him [Christ] in order that we may also be glorified with him" (Rom. 8:17); "For this light momentary affliction is preparing for us an eternal weight of glory beyond all comparison" (2 Cor. 4:17).

The Word of God's Mouth

But if God uses his hand in providence to put a touch of glory into our lives, he also transforms us as he speaks to us through Scripture. It is, after all, "the mouth of God" (Deut. 8:3; Matt. 4:4). And as our Christian forefathers understood, perhaps better than we do now, he does this especially through the preaching of the word as it is expounded and applied to us in the grace and power of the Spirit.[5]

Paul makes a telling comment about preaching when he gives thanks that the Thessalonians have "received the word of God, which you heard from us . . . not as the word of men but as what it really is, the word of God" (1 Thess. 2:13). And then he adds that this word "is *at work* in you believers."

These simple words contain an entire theology of preaching. It is therefore important that those who preach to us understand them, and that all of us as believers experience what they are describing—the word of God doing its own work in our lives.

Christians sometimes think of preaching in the following way:

- Preaching first of all tells us what God has done for us.
- Preaching then also tells us what we are to do in response.

5   See the Westminster Shorter Catechism, 89, and the Larger Catechism, 155.

First, pastors and teachers are reminded of their responsibility to preach and expound God's word in this fourfold way, because through such preaching, God works—individually, privately, and profoundly—on those who hear. Thus every exposition of Scripture is an extended personal counseling session in which the Holy Spirit shows us the wonder and power of the gospel and also exposes the secrets of our hearts. Preaching is not merely information being communicated by word of mouth. The exposition of a passage of Scripture is not intended to be a popular-level commentary in spoken form but an encounter with the God who speaks. For that reason, the preacher must be the hearer of his sermons even while he is preaching them. For, in the last analysis, it is Christ himself who preaches his own word through preachers. No surprise, then, that "a man preacheth that sermon only well unto others which preacheth itself in his own soul. . . . If the word do not dwell with power *in* us, it will not pass with power *from* us."[6]

Second, this explains why it is so important for us to place our lives under the influence of a living ministry of the word of God. We cannot produce by ourselves what

6 John Owen, *The Works of John Owen*, vol. 16, *The Church and the Bible*, ed. William H. Goold (1853; repr., London: Banner of Truth, 1968), 76.

God has planned to produce in us through the impact of the preaching of his word. If we try to, we are likely to become so used to being poorly nourished that we no longer notice it. That will certainly be true if the preaching we hear is less than biblical. We think we are doing fine—until in God's providence we encounter biblical preaching. Then we can taste the difference—so long as we have not fallen foul of the warning in Hebrews and have lost our sense of taste.[7]

When we hear the word of God expounded in the grace and power of the Holy Spirit, we are listening to the voice of the Good Shepherd himself calling his sheep. He has promised to illumine and renew our thinking, to expose our sin so that we may see, feel, and confess it, and experience its forgiveness. It is through preaching that Christ will heal our hurts and strengthen us to live for the glory of God. In a nutshell, his word itself will help us to live lives that are "worthy of the gospel" and create in us a reflection of Christ. For preaching is God's instrument by which "we all, with unveiled face, beholding the glory of the Lord, are being transformed into the same image, from one degree of glory to another. For this comes from the Lord who is the Spirit"

7   See Heb. 5:11–14.

(2 Cor. 3:18). And the Spirit loves to do this through the exposition of Scripture.

I doubt if anyone can understand this who has not experienced it. But when it is experienced, transformation takes place. But what does that look like? To that question we now turn.

4

A Worthy Mindset

What It Looks Like

IT IS ALL VERY WELL TO SAY that being "worthy of the gospel of Christ" means being restored to the image of God so that we begin to reflect the character of the Lord Jesus. But what does that mean?

The New Testament does not leave us to make this up. It does not allow us to say, "The way I like to think about this is . . ." In fact a few verses after urging his friends in Philippi to "be worthy," Paul explains that it means "have this mind among yourselves which is yours in Christ Jesus . . ." (Phil. 2:5).

To "be worthy" involves sharing "the mind [or as we might say, mindset] of Christ Jesus." Paul proceeds to explain that mindset in Philippians 2:5–11. True, these verses describe Christ's *actions*. But those actions are the expressions of his *mindset*—and sharing it is fundamental to living in a way that is "worthy of the gospel of Christ." Paul has the same goal in view when he later writes that those who are "mature" will think the same way he does (Phil. 3:15).

What then does it mean to have the mind of Christ?

A Model of Humility

I rarely think about Philippians 2:1–11 without recalling an evening in my first few weeks as a university student. I was seated in an Inter-Varsity meeting listening to the distinguished Anglican preacher John R. W. Stott expounding this passage.

He began calmly with a question: "What is the secret of Christian unity?" But then (to my horror!) he paused, waiting for one of us to answer. At age seventeen you don't have masses of wisdom, but I had enough to think, "I'm not answering him; I might get it wrong!" In fact, the first person to answer got it wrong, and so John Stott put us out of our misery. We waited in anticipation as he said, "The secret of Christian unity is"—I can still hear his refined Rugby School and Cambridge-educated accent pronounce the word—"humility."

Decades later, on the last occasion I heard him preach, I remembered his words. He was then experiencing TIAs,[1] and, having lost his place in the middle of his exposition, he stood quietly, and in a sense helpless, before the congregation. Hitherto I had never heard him miss a beat or struggle for words, the way ordinary preaching mortals do. But as John Stott now stood, dignified, but speechless for a few moments that may have seemed an eternity, I found myself transported in memory to that room where I, aged seventeen, heard him pronounce the word "humility." And I thought, "Now you are illustrating the humility of Christ about which you once taught us."

In the intervening years I had been befriended by him and had come to know him, and so I found his modeling of his own preaching very moving.

Perhaps you have had the privilege of knowing Christians who have left the same impression on you. According to Paul we are to watch them and to imitate them: "Brothers, join in imitating me, and keep your eyes on those who walk according to the example you have in us" (Phil. 3:17).

But what is it we have seen in these models? It is Christlikeness, isn't it? And the quintessence of this is humility—the mindset of the Savior.

---

1 A TIA is a transient ischemic attack, a mild but temporary stroke.

Imitation Is Not "Cloning"

Perhaps this is an appropriate place to include a word of warning. The biblical principle of imitating others is not a matter of "cloning." Biblical imitation means recognizing patterns and principles and building them into the way we ourselves do things. But if we try to be clones, we lose ourselves in the process—we never become the person we are cloning ourselves to be, nor are we any longer truly ourselves. And discerning eyes see through us. Genuine imitation is organic, not mechanical; it is internal, not external.

This warning has, perhaps, a special relevance to younger preachers. Certainly the danger—and perhaps the temptation—is most obvious in preachers because of their public role. Most people are not watched by anywhere between dozens and thousands of people each week!

I once heard an American preacher pass on a shrewd comment his preacher-father had made to him: "Many preachers spend the first five years of their ministry trying to be someone else, the next five years trying to find out who they really are, and the rest of their lives being the preacher the Lord meant them to be."

That's often true. And in some instances it is all too obviously true. Hence the warning: biblical *imitation* is not merely *external cloning*. It is not a matter of imitating mannerisms, intonations, phraseology, or idiosyncrasies. How oddly superficial to think that these are the source of a preacher's fruitfulness. Sometimes, of course, this is simply a matter of naivete. But sometimes it appears to be an attempt to take the fast route to usefulness; or even, sadly, impressiveness or influence. It is not always well motivated. Like Simon Magus, we might desire the fruit someone else displays without being willing to nurture the root, the trunk, or the branches of being in Christ ourselves.

When someone persists in cloning himself to be what he isn't, he ceases to be the person God means him to be. And the situation is worse if cloning is the—doubtless unspoken— goal of the institution in which he is trained. Then it may take either a crisis or an expert analyst to restore the reality of grace that leads to lasting fruitfulness.

Perhaps you have seen this, or even been this—someone who has lost himself in an effort to possess what another has. In the case of preaching, you may even recognize the preacher someone is attempting to be; or you sense the telltale signs of a lack of authenticity. It is a kind of act, a performance before us, rather than a spiritual nourishing. What is missing is the foot-washing disposition that comes from humility and love. There is a difference between the preaching of someone who is, in disposition, on his knees before you and someone who is on his feet lording it over you. Sadly, the difference is not always recognized. But the one is serving you while the other is using you—and perhaps even abusing you.

No doubt some of the characteristics of preachers we admire "rub off." But if so, we need to dust ourselves down. Otherwise, while we may not become false preachers, we nevertheless may become false as preachers. And then we will need to be further deconstructed if our ministry is to be "worthy of the gospel of Christ." We may not have plagiarized in order to impress others with a sermon that is not our own. But we may have plagiarized a character or personality others have in order to fulfill our ambition to possess another's reputation or ministry impact.

What is the missing note? Humility. We have wanted something God has not given us and tried to obtain it by being someone he has not made us to be. We may not have grasped equality with God, but we have grasped equality with someone else. It is un-Jesus-like. And almost inevitably, what is missing is the key Paul said opened a door into the hearts of the Thessalonians: "So, *being affectionately desirous of you, we were ready to share with you not only the gospel of God but also our own selves*, because you had become very dear to us" (1 Thess. 2:8).

If we have lost ourselves by becoming clones of someone else, it is not likely to be because we love God's people the way our loving Lord Jesus did, who "made himself of no reputation" (Phil. 2:7 KJV). Being "worthy of the gospel" as its heralds therefore requires the ability to echo (*properly imitate*) Paul's words in 2 Corinthians 4:5: "For what we proclaim is not ourselves, but Jesus Christ as Lord, *with ourselves as your servants for Jesus' sake*." Paul preached Christ as Lord. But what lent authenticity to his preaching was being like Jesus himself in the upper room: when Paul preached, he was inwardly on his knees before those who heard him. Far from seeking to be someone whose gifts they admired, he saw himself as their bondservant, whose service he wanted them to receive.

On Imitating Christ

So, humility is the mark of the worthy life because it is an authentic imitation of Christ. Of course, we are not in the form of God, nor do we literally face the death of the cross. But we are called to "have this mind among yourselves, which is yours in Christ Jesus" (Phil. 2:5). And in the words that follow, we are given a rare glimpse of what that means:

Who, though he was in the form of God,
did not count equality with God
a thing to be grasped,

But [he] emptied himself,
by taking the form of a servant,
being born in the likeness of men.

And being found in human form,
he humbled himself
by becoming obedient to the point of death,
even death on a cross. (Phil. 2:6–8 reformatted)

This, incidentally, explains why "God has highly exalted him" (Phil. 2:9). For God truly exalts only those who can be trusted with exaltation because their mindset is one of humility.

One of the ways in which this humble-mindedness comes to expression is in self-forgetfulness. It is what Anna Laetitia Waring described as

A heart at leisure from itself,
To soothe and sympathise.[2]

---

2   Anna Laetitia Waring, "Father I Know That All My Life" (1850).

It is worth noting that Paul almost immediately illustrates this in Philippians 2, in his moving description of his young colleague Timothy: "I have no one like him, who will be genuinely concerned for your welfare" (v. 20). By contrast, others "seek their own interests, not those of Jesus Christ" (v. 21). Paul goes on: "But you know Timothy's *proven worth*, how as a son with a father *he has served with me in the gospel*" (v. 22). Timothy was a model of a life that is worthy of the gospel because he shared the mindset of Christ. And because he shared Christ's mindset, he had begun to share Christ's likeness.

But if becoming "worthy of the gospel" means becoming more like Christ, we must ask a further question, one we need to ponder frequently: *What is the Lord Jesus really like?*

True Christlikeness

How can we answer that question? A good place to start is by remembering the words of Hebrews 13:8: "Jesus Christ is the same yesterday and today and forever."

This is not simply an elongated way of saying "Christ is Eternal." "Forever" does mean through all eternity. But "yesterday" does not mean "the day before today." It is the equivalent of the phrase, used earlier in Hebrews, "in the days of his flesh" (5:7). It refers to our Lord's earthly life. And "today" means not "the day after yesterday" but the "today" talked about earlier (6:6–13)—the whole time between Christ's first and second comings.

The point is this: Jesus Christ is now highly exalted at the right hand of God the Father. He is no longer humiliated and shamed, but glorified. *Yet he has not changed in himself.* He is still the same Jesus we read about in the Gospels. He is still today exactly what he said he was then. So our being worthy of his gospel means being like the very same Jesus about whom we read in the Gospels. And the way we become worthy is by imitating him, both consciously and unconsciously, by growing *down* in our estimation of ourselves so that we may grow *up* in humility.

Perhaps you are familiar with a saying of Augustine that John Calvin borrowed and developed:

When a certain rhetorician was asked what was the chief rule in eloquence, he replied, "Delivery"; what was the second rule, "Delivery"; what was the third rule, "Delivery"; so if you ask me concerning the precepts of the Christian religion, first, second, third, and always I would answer, "Humility."[3]

3 Augustine, quoted in John Calvin, *Institutes of the Christian Religion*, ed. John T. McNeill, trans. Ford Lewis Battles (Philadelphia; Westminster, 1960), 2.2.11. The rhetorician to whom reference is made here was the Greek orator Demosthenes.

Think of how Jesus's humble mindset was revealed in the actions the Gospels record—his willingness to become one of us in all the smallness of baby humanity; to share all the trials, afflictions, and disappointments of life; to wash the dirty feet of his disciples; and then to be willing to take our shame on the cross of Calvary.

Think too of what was written about him:

> He will not quarrel or cry aloud,
>   nor will anyone hear his voice in the streets;
> a bruised reed he will not break,
>   and a smoldering wick he will not quench.
>   (Matt. 12:19–20 citing Isa. 42:2–3)

Or think of what he said of himself:

> Come to me, all who labor and are heavy laden, and I will give you rest. Take my yoke upon you, and learn from me, for I am gentle and lowly in heart, and you will find rest for your souls. For my yoke is easy, and my burden is light. (Matt. 11:28–30)

There's a through-and-through humility here. That is what attracted people to the Lord Jesus; that's why they knew instinctively they could go to him, open their hearts to him, and tell him their needs; that's why they entrusted themselves, their secrets, their sorrows, their disappointments in life to him. You don't do that with people who aren't humble-hearted. Only a humble heart is big enough both for itself and for you.

Remember how Paul opened his heart to the Corinthians who had closed their hearts to him? He appealed to them "by the meekness and gentleness of Christ" (2 Cor. 10:1). We don't know how much of the Gospels Paul knew—I suspect more than is often thought. But he was obviously familiar with these "comfortable words"[4] recorded of Jesus in Matthew 11:28–30.

This is what Jesus is like, and therefore this is what you are called to be like too. He himself is the gospel. A life that is "worthy" of that gospel, which corresponds to it, is a life that reflects him. This isn't incidental to living the Christian life; it is the goal of it, and in a sense, it is the whole of it. Everything else flows from it. Nothing else matters. And at the end of the day, only what is Christlike in your life and character will last for eternity.

Most Christians are familiar with Paul's majestic, assurance-filled words in Romans 8:28. They must rank in the top 1 percentile of all-time favorite Bible verses: "And we know that for those who love God all things work together for

---

4   To borrow an expression from the Book of Common Prayer.

good, for those who are called according to his purpose." But Paul hadn't completed his thought when he said the word "purpose." Here is how he finished it: "For those whom he foreknew he also predestined to be conformed to the image of his Son, in order that he might be the firstborn among many brothers" (Rom. 8:29).

Our transformation into the likeness of Jesus Christ has been God's purpose for us from before the dawn of creation. It is central to his purposes for us. And he will stop at nothing to accomplish it. He will spare nothing to make you like his Son. We know that because, in order to accomplish it, "He . . . did not spare his own Son but gave him up for us all" (Rom. 8:32).

So, how shall we respond to Paul's exhortation to "live worthy"?

First of all, by praying: "Lord, make me more like Jesus. Conform me to his image. Write these words on my heart":

Let the beauty of Jesus be seen in me,
All his wonderful passion and purity,
O thou Spirit divine, all my nature refine,
Till the beauty of Jesus be seen in me.[5]

5   Albert W. T. Orsborn, "Let the Beauty of Jesus Be Seen in Me" (1916).

5

A Life Worthy

How It Came About—and Comes About

TO BE "WORTHY OF THE GOSPEL OF CHRIST" means becoming more like Jesus himself. We have seen that Paul urges us to commit ourselves to a new "manner of life." He goes on to tell us that this means that Christ's mindset is to become ours too. Thus humility is born.

If, as those who belong to Christ, who are "in Christ," we are to become like Christ, how will that happen?

We have already seen that this happens in part through the imitation of Christ. By a kind of spiritual osmosis we begin to imitate what we have seen and heard, and gradually it becomes our own.

The Scent of Worthiness

Elsewhere Paul hints that Christians have an aroma about them. In the metaphorical sense, we all do. Our lives, personalities, dispositions, actions, and words all combine to create a kind of atmosphere in our lives, a scent in the air that surrounds us.

We sometimes describe people as "odorous." We speak about other people as "sweet" or "pleasant." Someone gets into the elevator, and when he leaves, you realize from the atmosphere that he must have been smoking a cigarette. Someone else passes you by, and seconds later you realize he is wearing cologne. These impressions may change, depending on what someone is wearing, has been smoking or cooking, and so forth. But in a thousand little ways we are constantly breathing out, or giving expression to, who and what we really are. Try to disguise it we may; hide it we never can.

During my days in elementary school in Scotland, each morning a crate of milk bottles was brought into the classroom. The government had decreed what we all called "milk time," and we duly stopped our work and sucked our rations of milk through paper straws. Years later I was amused to read a Japanese man commenting that to him all Scottish people smelled of milk! "No wonder," I thought, "considering the quantities we drank in our childhood!" But none of us ever noticed it.

Something similar is true in the Christian life, isn't it? None of us knows exactly what aroma we leave behind when we walk out of a room or finish a conversation. And it is true that, like perfumes or aftershaves, there is no guarantee other people will be able to identify the aroma and give it a name. But the life that is worthy of the gospel inevitably leaves behind a gospel aroma, the scent of the Lord Jesus. For there is something about Christlike humility that cannot be explained in any other way than likeness to him. A life that "matches" the gospel, and is therefore "worthy" of it, always leaves behind the aroma of his presence.

How does this come about? We have already seen that when Paul gives the exhortation to "be worthy," he also explains what it means and how it comes about. It should not really surprise us, then, that he also indicates how this happened in his own life and describes his experience as a working model for others.

Saul of Tarsus Discovers a Worthy Life

When we first meet Saul of Tarsus, the Roman citizen, his goal was what he considered to be a "worthy" manner of life. From his earliest days he had been nurtured in being worthy, and as he grew he had deliberately cultivated it, though in a misguided way.

When he was writing to the church at Philippi, Paul (as, by then, he was known) was concerned about a group of false teachers with a Jewish background. They were insisting that anyone who wanted to belong to God's chosen people needed to be marked with the ancient sign of circumcision that God had given to Abraham and his seed.[1] The apostle was warning his friends that this false teaching was simply another form of "confidence in the flesh" (Phil. 3:3).

Although by this time Paul looked back on his earlier life with a deep sense of sadness and shame, he also realized that on this occasion it providentially stood him in good stead. For he shared the same personal history as these opponents of the gospel; he knew exactly where they were going wrong, and how to correct it.

Not only so, but if people wanted to boast in the purity of their pedigree and their religious performance, they had met their match in him: "If anyone else thinks he has reason for confidence in the flesh, I have more" (Phil. 3:4).

---

1   For our purposes here it is not necessary to decide whether these were Jews who had a conscious strategy to oppose Paul's ministry or "Judaizers" who insisted that circumcision and other Mosaic ordinances be continued in a mandatory fashion in all the churches.

That wasn't boasting; it was a simple fact.

A friend once hosted me and some others to a lunch in a famous club in London. The walls were covered with portraits of some of the great figures from the past. Looking around at them, I lightheartedly said to our host, "I suppose you are related to some of these people." He smiled and nodded in the direction of one of the portraits. But it was of the eighteenth-century prime minister of Great Britain William Pitt the Elder, whose son (who became the youngest ever British prime minister) was a close friend of William Wilberforce. Here I was—brought up in the east end of Glasgow—standing next to a descendant of a British prime minister! It was, of course, a wonderful illustration that there is neither Scot nor English in Christ. But in the presence of my friend none of his guests could boast of their pedigree!

No one could out-boast Paul when it came to pedigree. But there was something more: neither could they outrun him when it came to performance. He had committed himself to the strictest sect of the Jews, the Pharisees. And if that were not already an indication of his "zeal" for God's law, he added to it, in his own estimation, by becoming "a persecutor of the church" (Phil. 3:6).

But now, compared with knowing Christ as his Lord, everything he had counted as gain he saw as "loss," indeed as "rubbish" (Phil. 3:7–8).

What happened? Our instinct is perhaps to answer, "The Damascus road experience." But the story is more complex than that. It is worth exploring, because it gives us some clues to what Paul has in mind when he speaks about living "worthy of the gospel of Christ."

We need to go back to the beginning of the story of Saul of Tarsus.

Where was he spiritually?

Saul had chosen to belong to "the strictest party" of the Jews (Acts 26:5). He was a Pharisee. But by no means were all Pharisees church persecutors. Gamaliel, the highly respected member of the Sanhedrin and Saul's own theology professor in Jerusalem (Acts 22:3), was also a Pharisee. But he had counseled *against* persecuting the church (Acts 5:33–39). So, what happened—first, to ignite Saul's desire to destroy Christ's church (Acts 8:3) and, then, to transform his desire into knowing and serving Christ whatever the cost?

Clues to Saul's Zeal and Transformation

While it may be impossible to be dogmatic about it, several clues help us piece together his whole story.

The first clue is found in Galatians 1. Looking back on his early years, Paul says, "I was advancing in Judaism beyond many of my own age among my people, so extremely zealous was I for the traditions of my fathers" (v. 14). That is almost certainly a slightly embarrassed way of recalling, "I was the religious numero uno; I was determined nobody would better me."

The second clue is in Philippians 3. At that earlier time, at least in his own view, Paul was, "as to righteousness under the law, blameless" (vv. 4–6; the rich young ruler in the Gospels seems to have felt exactly the same about himself—Luke 18:18–21).

The third clue appears in Acts 6. Against the background of a period of tension in the Jerusalem church, Luke focuses, in Acts 6:8, on a young man whose presence dominates the two chapters that follow—Stephen. Like Saul's other name *Paulus, Stephanos* is not a Hebrew name. Perhaps they were both "outsiders."

In any event, Christ had given Stephen remarkable gifts. He had a fivefold fullness. He was "full . . . of *wisdom*" and "full of *faith* and of *the Holy Spirit*" (Acts 6:3, 5). In addition, he was "full *of power*" and "full . . . *of grace*" (Acts 6:8). As becomes clear, he also had a tremendous grasp of the teaching of the Hebrew Bible and was skilled in showing how its message prepared the way for, and pointed to, the coming of the Savior. As a result of preaching this, Stephen was singled out for persecution.

Just at this point Luke injects information into his narrative that slows everything down for a moment. He provides a detailed list of the makeup of the synagogue that formed the epicenter of the opposition to Stephen: "The synagogue of the Freedmen (as it was called), and of the Cyrenians, and of the Alexandrians, and of those from Cilicia and Asia, rose up and disputed with Stephen" (Acts 6:9).

We tend to gloss over these words to get to the main point: "But they could not withstand the wisdom and the Spirit with which he was speaking" (Acts 6:10). But why these details? They seem to add nothing to the story, and they slow down the pace of the unfolding drama. Is this a literary blunder on Luke's part? It might seem so to a literary critic, and most of us simply race past it.

But when something that doesn't need to be there is there, it is usually there for a reason! Here Luke is slowing down the narrative to get us to stop and reflect so that we will later remember. He is giving us a key to something that is still to come. For in Acts 9:11, he will tell us that Saul (who, by Acts 6, has not yet appeared on the scene) was from Tarsus.

Now Tarsus was in Cilicia. Since Jews from outside Jerusalem seem to have joined themselves to ethnic synagogues in the city, this synagogue that led the opposition to Stephen was almost certainly the one Saul attended. And since its members came from the Hellenistic world, perhaps this was also the synagogue to which Stephanos had once belonged.

When we connect these dots, a picture begins to emerge.

It seems to have been with the emergence of Stephen and the powerful public display of his spiritual gifts that, probably for the first time in his life, Saul of Tarsus met a contemporary who was his superior in all the things that really mattered to him: knowledge of the Bible, righteousness, zeal, and a grace-filled, Holy Spirit–empowered life.

If so, this helps to explain a final clue.

The fourth clue is found in Romans 7. As Paul reflects on his past life, he says, "I was once alive apart from the law, but when the commandment came, sin came alive and I died" (v. 9). He makes an interesting distinction here between "the law" (as a whole), and "the commandment." In fact, he has just indicated that he has in mind the tenth commandment in particular: "You shall not covet" (v. 7). He adds, "Sin, seizing an opportunity through the commandment, produced in me all kinds of covetousness" (v. 8). It is *in this context* that he tells us, "I was once alive apart from the law, but when the commandment came, sin came alive and I died" (v. 9).

Why does he single out this commandment in particular?

One common answer is that he does so because this, the last commandment in the Decalogue, deals with inward motivation. That is true. But all the commandments imply inward motivation. Another explanation is surely necessary. Something must have happened in Saul's life to make him recognize the covetousness in his heart—something he perhaps never before experienced in the same profound way. Now, as a result, "sin came alive and I died" (v. 9).

No wonder, for (surely deliberately) Luke describes no one in more Christlike terms than Stephen.[2]

Saul of Tarsus approved of Stephen's martyrdom by stoning (Acts 8:1; see also 7:58). At the time, Saul was in no state of mind to analyze and understand what was happening to him. But it seems clear enough: for the first time in his life he had met someone who had what he lacked, although he had striven for it all his life: wisdom, the Holy Spirit, righteousness, a profound grasp of God's truth and an ability to explain and apply it, unmistakable evidence of the hand of God in his life, and that so highly prized quality—grace. So Saul of Tarsus was now faced with two alternatives: to ask Stephen how to attain what he had but

2 Luke brings this out in very definite ways in Acts 6:5a, 8, 10, 15; 7:55–60.

Saul lacked—to humble himself and seek Christ—or angrily to try to destroy the cause of his covetousness. Saul chose the latter. And in doing so, he saw a man whose eyes were fixed on Christ.

It wasn't only *the triumphant death* of Stephen that affected Saul. It was the *Christlikeness of Stephen's life.* He almost certainly provided the clearest, if not the first, glimpse of Christ that Saul of Tarsus ever had.

I suspect that whenever Paul later thought about Christlikeness, he remembered Stephen. You can understand why he never refers to him directly: Paul's participation in his martyrdom must have been a wound he carried to his grave. And so he left the telling of the story to his friend Luke. But Luke makes clear there was a definite connection between the death of Stephen and the conversion of Saul. Stephen was like the grain of wheat that falls into the earth and dies but, as a result, "bears much fruit" (John 12:24).

Who could doubt that Stephen lived in a way that was "worthy of the gospel of Christ"?

It should not really surprise us, then, that the significance of Christlikeness runs deep in Paul's teaching. Here too we can detect the fingerprints of Stephen. Indeed, to perhaps a surprising degree, much of Paul's teaching can be traced back to this womb in which his own faith in Christ was conceived.

But before we develop this, it is worth pausing to notice another feature of this story.

The Humble Servant behind the Scenes

While some individuals have roles in the church that seem head and shoulders above others, the truth is much more complex. The New Testament devotes comparatively little space to Stephen. (Were it not for the Acts of the Apostles, we would not even know of his existence.) But it devotes much space to Paul. And even the space Stephen occupies in Acts can seem excessive to readers who trudge through his extended piece of biblical theology in Acts 7 and want to rush on to Saul's conversion. But in God's economy, Stephen is the sine qua non of that conversion. The Christlikeness of his life is the blueprint for Paul's teaching. The man who remains relatively obscure, and indeed disappears in the story, really matters.

That is a standing principle in the way God establishes and extends his kingdom. To make the point, try this exam question: The following seven men have been major figures and profoundly influential in the church in the past five hundred years. Beside each, name the person who had the greatest spiritual influence on him.

MAJOR FIGURES	INFLUENCED BY
Martin Luther	
John Calvin	
John Owen	
Jonathan Edwards	
George Whitefield	
Charles Haddon Spurgeon	
D. Martyn Lloyd-Jones	

These are all well-known individuals. But most of us would probably have to leave several answers blank. Either we don't know, or perhaps nobody knows who most influenced them. Yet, humanly speaking, these unknown influencers were essential links in the chain of God's purposes. The history of the church looks like the story of a few giants; but it isn't. It goes much deeper and is much more complex. And it teaches us that what matters is not our prominence but our being faithful in the place and at the time God assigns to us. That requires a spirit of humble service, a "How can I serve others?" rather than an "Are my gifts being recognized by others?" disposition.

Some Christians are slow to grasp this last principle. They are more gift-conscious than self-forgetful. Among them are the kind of people who trouble pastors when they inquire about church membership: "If I join your church, will I be able to teach?" Sometimes it takes only a little judicious probing to discern that their first thought is not "I will serve wherever this church family needs me and thinks I can be useful" but "Will these people recognize my gift and create the space I need to showcase it?" Alas, whatever the abilities an individual may have, this is poorly disguised spiritual narcissism. Wanting to have a position and to teach or influence others is not the same as wanting to serve them.

Can you imagine our Lord discussing the incarnation with his Father and saying, "I'll join them—so long as they recognize my gifts"?

In sharp contrast, Jesus shows us that living in a way that "matches" or is "worthy" of the gospel means being willing to take the slave's role of kneeling before others and washing their dirty feet, with our hands full of love. It is the antithesis of wanting to tower over them so that they recognize who we are and what talents we have (John 13:14–15). It means being far more interested in giving ourselves to others than in having a position among them. That's what Jesus was like—he came not to be served but to serve and to give his life for others (Matt. 20:28).

The worthy life, then, is a life that becomes a connecting link between the Savior and others. And as we have seen, that means "humility, humility, humility."

Life through Death

Paul learned a further lesson from his encounter with Stephen: Christlikeness is produced by the pattern of Christ's death and resurrection being reproduced in his disciples. This is the ground plan on which the Christian life is built; this is the mold that shapes the new life in Christ. What Paul saw in Stephen finds a powerful echo in his words to the Corinthians: "We who live . . . are always being given over to death for Jesus' sake, so that the life of Jesus also may be manifested in our mortal flesh. *So death is at work in us, but life in you*" (2 Cor. 4:11–12).

"Death . . . at work in us, but life in you" would have been a fitting epitaph for Stephen. For the conversion of Saul of Tarsus and the ministry of Paul the apostle are the fruit of the death that worked in Stephen. And so union and communion with Christ in his death and resurrection became the lenses through which Paul saw the whole of his (and our) Christian life. He realized that becoming like Christ involved the imprinting of the same pattern Christ had imprinted on Stephen's life, whether in a minor or a major way. For the growth in the knowledge of Christ that leads to likeness to Christ is produced only in this Christlike way.

The centrality of this appears when we return to Paul's testimony in Philippians 3. His deepest aspiration became this: "that I may know him and the power of his resurrection, and may share his sufferings, becoming like him in his death, that by any means possible [i.e., whatever it takes] I may attain the resurrection from the dead" (Phil. 3:10–11).

Here again we encounter internal and external death and life, "mortification" and "vivification." Being a Christian involves participation in Christ's sufferings but also sharing in his triumphs. Since this is what it was like for God's Son, this is what it will also be like for those who are being "conformed to the image of his Son." There is no other way to reflect him.

The Spirit worked this out in the life of Stephen. Paul saw it, and by God's grace the same transformation began to take place in him. He wrote about how it happens. Through the written word we see and come to know the living Word. In him, as we "behold the glory of the Lord," we are "transformed into the same image from one degree of glory to another. For this comes from the Lord who is the Spirit" (2 Cor. 3:18).

Without this reflection of Christ we can never be "worthy of the gospel of Christ."

The Christian who discovers this blueprint in Scripture and experiences it for himself or herself will then be able to say with Paul that the whole focus of life is to "know him and the power of his resurrection, and . . . share his sufferings, becoming like him in his death, that by any means possible I may attain the resurrection from the dead" (Phil. 3:10–11). And that aspiration leads to this assurance: "Our citizenship is in heaven, and from it we await a Savior, the Lord Jesus Christ, who will transform our lowly body to be like his glorious body, by the power that enables him even to subject all things to himself" (Phil. 3:20–21). Growing Christlikeness now will give way to perfect Christlikeness then.

So What?

Reflecting on Paul's teaching here may leave us feeling this is an exceptional story but still asking the "So what?" question: What difference—if any—does all this actually make to my Christian life?

For Paul himself it led to a multifaceted transformation that affected every area of his life. The same will be true for us.

In the first place, the "worthy life" is marked by what we might call a "dissatisfied satisfaction." Now nothing can bring Paul greater satisfaction than knowing Christ. And yet, now that he has come to know Christ, he cannot rest satisfied. He has not yet attained everything he longs for. He knows Christ, but he wants to know him better (Phil. 3:12). He has experienced the presence of Christ and the love of Christ—but he cannot be satisfied until he experiences both more fully.

Second, the "worthy life" operates with a different spiritual accountancy. Paul's new "bottom line" is that for the sake of Christ he counts as loss what he once counted as a gain. The things he once boasted in—his pedigree and his performance—he now sees not simply as reduced to neutral value; he places them in the "loss column." Yes, he knew he had been given great privileges (see Rom. 3:1–2); but now he realizes he had missed their real point. He had failed to see how they all pointed to Christ. Instead he had used them to point to himself and to why he had no need of Christ.

But now Paul sees all that as "loss."

In fact he goes a step further. He now counts "*everything* as loss" for the sake of Christ. Paul may have meant that literally. Jewish believers who have gained Christ have often been disinherited by their families and left with no visible means of support. But if this was Paul's experience, he tells us that this loss was to his advantage; for, he says, "I have suffered the loss of all things and count them as rubbish, *in order that* I may gain Christ and be found in him" (Phil. 3:8–9).

One day, as a young theology student, I found myself reflecting on the various meanings of the Greek word *skybala*, translated in the ESV as "rubbish." I can still remember the slight shudder I felt on reading the words that concluded the entry in my Greek lexicon: "usually translated 'dung.'" Paul was not a world despiser. But by comparison with the riches he had found in Christ, the entire world without his Savior seemed no more valuable to him than excrement. After all, you could gain it all and lose your own soul (Matt. 16:26).

There was a third effect that Paul experienced, a single-minded simplicity: "One thing I do: . . . I press on toward the goal" (Phil. 3:13–14).

Both Paul and Timothy are mentioned in the opening greetings of this letter (Phil. 1:1). Even if Paul was not dictating the letter to Timothy, we can assume that Paul's son in the faith was at least in the room with him. Don't you think Timothy might have cleared his throat when the apostle said that he did "one thing"? I can imagine the younger man saying, rather gingerly: "Are you sure you want to put it that way, Paul? I've *never* seen you do *only one thing*. You always seem to be doing a dozen things!"

Paul did not see it that way. He was not doing a dozen things. He was doing one thing in a dozen ways. At the heart of everything he did was pressing on to know, trust, love, and serve his Lord Jesus Christ! That was only one thing—but it affected everything.

Here, then, is a radically different way to live.

Jesus Christ gives us a *new identity*; we are "in Christ," and as a result our lives are being shaped into his image by his word and Spirit. We are becoming like him. But in addition, he builds into our lives a *new integrity*, a single unifying principle that coordinates everything we do and makes all our endeavors aspects of one great reality—our union and communion with him. So, whatever we do, whether overtly "spiritual" or apparently not, whether studying at school or working in an office or a factory or a hospital or a university, whether running a company or being a homemaker or pastoring a church family—everything we do is done out of devotion to Christ and as a tribute to his grace. Our double vision on life is healed. Now we see things clearly, as they relate to Christ. There are no longer many disconnected activities to engage in but one great activity to pursue in a multiplicity of ways: knowing Christ and becoming like him.

In this way our lives increasingly become mirrors of the life of the Lord Jesus, in whom everything was integrated in his desire to love and please his heavenly Father in all things and thus to live for his glory.

This is what happens when we are "in Christ." He comes to mean so much to us that we can say, "I count everything as loss because of the surpassing worth of knowing Christ Jesus my Lord" (Phil. 3:8).

This, according to Paul, is how mature Christians think (Phil. 3:15).

And this is what leads to a "manner of life" that is "worthy of the gospel of Christ."

General Index

Scripture Index

Union

We fuel reformation in churches and lives.

Union Publishing invests in the next generation of leaders with theology that gives them a taste for a deeper knowledge of God. From books to our free online content, we are committed to producing excellent resources that will refresh, transform, and grow believers and their churches.

We want people everywhere to know, love, and enjoy God, glorifying him in everything they do. For this reason, we've collected hundreds of free articles, podcasts, book chapters, and video content for our free online collection. We also produce a fresh stream of written, audio, and video resources to help you to be more fully alive in the truth, goodness, and beauty of Jesus.

If you are hungry for reformational resources that will help you delight in God and grow in Christ, we'd love for you to visit us at unionpublishing.org.

unionpublishing.org

Also Available in the Growing Gospel Integrity Series

This series invites readers to pursue spiritual growth through four marks of integrity: worthy lives, unity, courage, and humility. Each book examines one of these marks—why they are essential, what they should look like, how the gospel molds these qualities, and how individuals and churches can be shaped by them. Through this series, Christians will be challenged to grow in spiritual integrity, rejoicing in and living by the gospel they profess.

For more information, visit **crossway.org**.